AMERICA'S RAILROAD STATIONS

AMERICA'S RAILROAD STATIONS

Text and photographs by
BRIAN SOLOMON

GRAMERCY BOOKS
NEW YORK

This 2002 edition is published by Gramercy™ Books, an imprint of Random House Value Publishing, Inc., 280 Park Avenue, New York, NY 10017.

Gramercy™ Books and design are trademarks of Random House Value Publishing, Inc.

Random House
New York • Toronto • London • Sydney • Auckland
www.randomhouse.com

Editor: Celeste Sollod
Art director: Christine Kell
Interior designer: Carol Malcolm Russo/Signet M Design, Inc.

Printed and bound in Singapore

A catalog record for this title is available from the Library of Congress.

ISBN 0-517-22001-6

10 9 8 7 6 5 4 3 2 1

All photographs by Brian Solomon unless otherwise credited:

Page 2: Philadelphia Broad Street Station: postcard courtesy of Seán Solomon; Boston South Street Station: postcard courtesy of Richard Jay Solomon

Pages 3 and 4: photos by William Bullard, courtesy of Dennis Lebeau

Pages 5 and 7: photos by William D. Middleton

Page 15: Harrisburg, PA, train shed: photo by Richard Jay Solomon

Page 46: Bellows Falls, VT, conductor: photo by Richard Jay Solomon

Page 48: photo by Richard Jay Solomon

To my brother, Seán Solomon

Acknowledgments

I'm always thrilled to visit a railway station and I always enjoy seeking out new stations in the course of my travels. My brother Seán has often accompanied me on railway trips, and we've spent more than two decades exploring stations around America. Many people have helped me over the years in my unceasing quest for photos and information on railways past and present. Among those who helped me with the photography and research that went into this book are: Robert A. Buck of Tucker's Hobbies, John Gruber, Mel Patrick, Mike Gardner, Brian Jennison, Tom Danneman, Tim Doherty, George Pitarys, John P. Hankey, George C. Corey, Doug Moore, Paul Hammond, and my good friends the Hoover family. Special thanks to my father, Richard Jay Solomon, for the use of his library and lending me his photographs, and my mother, Maureen Solomon, for many small tasks including driving me to railway stations on numerous occasions and sorting my mail during my many lengthy trips. Thanks also to William D. Middleton, who has lent me photographs, and who himself has authored several of my favorite books on railways; Dennis Lebeau, who lent me photos from the William Bullard archive; the Irish Railway Record Society for the use of their facilities; and the helpful folks at the Denver Public Library for their assistance with photo research.

Introduction:
A Nation of Stations

Today a railway station conveys romantic visions of the past. It was here at the station that we set off on our summer holidays, said good bye to soldiers heading off to war, or bid farewell to the loves of our lives before beginning the journey that would change us forever. The maelstrom of activity of the big city station distilled the wonder, mystique, and energy of the city itself, while the small town depot embodied the quaint charm of country life. Arrival at a big union station or terminal to change trains represented a crossroads. While most travelers made their connections as planned, there was always a chance, serendipitous or calculated, that you might change direction. Instead of heading east to visit a maiden aunt, you might catch a limited for the Coast to seek your fortune. While pondering such travel dilemmas, you could pause to have your shoes shined, pick up a local paper, get a haircut, telegraph home for advice, snack at the railway restaurant, or even take a bath.

For more than a hundred years railroad travel was simply the best way to go. The pulse of the United States was measured by the activity of the railroads. Railroads carried people to and from work; sent them on long trips for business and pleasure; and carried heavy freight, express shipments, and the mail. The railroad facilitated the settlement, development, and prosperity of the country.

For the average person the station was the focal point of railroad activity. In a really small town, the mere arrival of the train was an event in itself. The trains

Opposite: New York's Grand Central Terminal is probably the best known railway terminal in the world. When the station was completed in 1913, it was designed to accommodate a much greater volume of passengers than passed through it at that time. When peak railway travel finally occurred 30 years later, Grand Central's spacious design proved fit for the task its designers intended. In the late 1990s, the station was renovated, allowing the world to see its beauty and charm. The floor of the grand concourse is made of Tennessee Marble, while the ceiling is a parabolic dome with a reverse interpretation of the evening sky, complete with hundreds of lit stars.

Above, top: *The Pennsylvania Railroad's Broad Street Station in Philadelphia was one of the great nineteenth-century American terminals. It featured the largest single span train shed ever built, and an ornate brick head house designed by Frank Furness. The shed was destroyed by fire in 1923, and the head was closed in 1952 and later demolished.*

Above, bottom: *Boston's South Station's magnificent façade was the work of Shepley, Rutan and Coolidge. For many years this terminal was the busiest passenger station in the United States. In 1904, South Station served 861 trains daily. The elevated railway in front of the station was removed in 1942.*

brought everything one needed from the outside world, from goods to news. Anyone of any importance came and went by train.

In larger towns or those on busy trunk lines—the main lines that carried railway traffic from east to west and back again—the parade of trains seemed endless. There were the early morning and evening passenger locals that brought people to and from the city for work, and the fancy long-distance luxury-limiteds with their varnished Pullman sleepers, deluxe diners, and open-air observation cars that raced cross-country at high speeds. Anyone might be riding on these fast trains: visiting royalty, a great musician, or a star of the silver screen. Local freights rolled into town and paused at the station to switch freight cars. These trains, often running between the scheduled trains, would pull into sidings to make way for the fast freights and slower moving drags. These were long trains of freight cars that carried everything from livestock and fresh fruit to the products of industry. Then there were the daily scheduled milk runs that collected fresh milk in the morning and brought it to the cities for processing and distribution. Often these slow-moving trains carried passengers, too. In the middle of the night, the mail trains raced through, picking up mail and dropping it off "on the fly," that is, without stopping.

Trains and the station agent were the link from smaller towns to the outside world in the days before the advent of private automobiles, super highways, and home telecommunications. The agent would sell you your tickets and give you the proper time, and could also tell if your favorite team won the pennant, or if the price for cattle feed was up or down. It's amazing what the agent could find out by tapping the telegraph key and listening to the wire. It was all part of the romance of the railway station.

These days, a railway station, when you find one, is too often just a reminder of the way things were. The station that was once so important may now be just a derelict building in a bad part of town. In many cases it is simply gone. It may have been demolished years ago following a fire, or perhaps the railway needed space for a parking lot, or maybe it was costing the line too much in taxes and the accountants thought the company could do better without it. Some stations survive and a few are now handsomely restored, but often they no longer serve the purpose for which they were built. They might be offices, shops, or private residences.

However, in recent times, more and more stations have been properly restored and are being used as railway stations again, such as the fine stations at Worcester, Massachusetts (see pages 26–29); Washington D.C. (see pages 22–25); and Los Angeles, California (see page 7). In many cities the once decrepit, sometimes abandoned, depot has been fully restored to its former glory. While American railways are no longer as important as they once were, railway travel never died out all together, and in many places it has been renewed and again has a viable place in the modern world. With clogged highways, rising fuel costs, long commutes, and traffic, taking the train is often the best way to go!

The Beauty of the Station

One of the pleasures of American railway travel is viewing the seemingly limitless diversity in railway architecture. An estimated 80,000 to 85,000 stations were constructed in the United States. In addition to passenger depots, there were thousands of supporting structures such as switch towers, engine houses, car shops, railroad offices, and railroad hotels. The great variety of architectural styles applied to these buildings was the result of a myriad of influences on railway station design. The earliest American stations date to the 1830s, while the most

Below, top: It has been many years since a passenger train called on the Illinois Central station at Zachary, Louisiana, yet the tracks still host the railroad's freight trains.

Below, bottom: Many of the tens of thousands of railway stations in the United States were just small halting sites like this tiny station at Quinapoxet, Massachusetts. Sadly, many of these quaint small depots were the first to go when railroad traffic began to slump. This view dates from the turn of the twentieth century.

recent are still being built. During these seventeen decades of railway station construction, there has been an evolution in architectural styles. Geographical influences, the demands of the public, and the individual needs and desires of the railroad companies have all contributed to the various styles of individual stations along American railway lines.

The large number of railroad companies in the United States played a great role in diversity of style and adornment used in railway station design. In the nineteenth century there were hundreds of different railroad companies, and each wanted stations distinguishable from those of its competitors. A prosperous railroad wanted to show off its wealth, both to appease the demands of the public and demonstrate that the company was well-run and worthy of investment. Some lines had architects design groups of similar-looking stations. The common

Above: As railroads became more prosperous they built nicer and more substantial stations along their lines. The Boston & Albany hired Henry Hobson Richardson, one of the best-known architects of his day, to design many of its stations. Richardson only actively participated in the design of a few B&A stations, leaving many to his associates, Shepley, Rutan and Coolidge, who held true to the theme he had established. This station at Huntington, Massachusetts, was completed in 1892 at the cost of $9,001.

architectural characteristics would give passengers a sense of continuity when traveling over the line. The Boston & Albany hired the famous American architect Henry Hobson Richardson to design their stations. Following his untimely death in 1886, his successors continued his work, creating railroad stations in the Richardson Romanesque style for the B&A as well as other lines in the region. In a similar vein, the Baltimore & Ohio employed E. Francis Baldwin and his partner Josias Pennington to design many of the structures along its lines.

As railroads merged and consolidated, with bigger companies buying up smaller ones, the new management might deem older stations unsuitable for the traffic or image of the new line. Because railroads continually upgraded their facilities, very few early railroad buildings exist in America today. Most existing American stations were built after the Civil War. A few early stations have survived, such as the one in Ellicott City, Maryland, the oldest remaining station in the United States.

Not all companies had the resources or the desire to employ distinguished architects. Some railroads, particularly those operating in the Midwest and Great Plains regions, were noted for their comparatively minimalist station designs. These were often built to standard plans drawn up by company civil engineers. A railroad might have four or five standard depot designs of varying sizes that would be used for stations along the line. A standard plan would dictate the basic dimensions and arrangement of the station building, but would leave flexible such details as door and window placement, and the location of platforms as well as simple styling. These details would be designed to suit the particular town for which the station was built. Midwestern depots built to those standard plans are usually small wooden stations. Often railroads couldn't justify the cost of more permanent-looking stations in growing villages and towns along their lines.

However, as result of rapid growth, a town might soon find that the station erected in the first days of the railroad had become outmoded. If a town prospered, a more substantial depot could be built. Some towns may have had as many as four or five stations successively at the same location. The stone and brick stations found all across America today were often built as replacement stations. These were typically of a nicer design than the

Above: The Atlantic Coast Line's Everglades *is seen pausing at Broad Street Station in Richmond, Virginia, on September 13, 1957. The Atlantic Coast Line operated its trains from cities in Florida to Richmond. From here the trains continued northward over the Richmond, Fredericksburg & Potomac line to Washington D.C. and then to New York over the Pennsylvania Railroad.*

simple wooden stations, but still might follow a standard floor plan and be designed for just a few trains a day without any complicated facilities. The red brick and stone depot at Whitewater, Wisconsin (see pages 60–61), built in 1890, is one such building. Modest but well-built, it was designed to replace an earlier wooden frame depot constructed in 1852.

More important towns, such as a county seat, state capitol, or the site of a significant junction, warranted more substantial stations than those in the smaller towns. Here architects were given more creative license, and money was spent more liberally on materials, construction and decoration, especially on later stations built after a railroad had established itself financially and had become an important part of a community.

Regional influences are very evident in the types of architecture chosen for railway station design. The great variety of architectural styles of American stations is in part product of the country's vast geography and the many different influences on American architecture. Stations in the Southwest are noted for their Spanish influence; those in the Northeast are characterized by Classical touches. American stations have displayed Greek Revival, Romanesque, Gothic Revival, Tudor, Colonial, Beaux-Arts, and Art Deco architecture.

For its relatively small size, New England has one of the most diverse collections of railroad stations. In Connecticut alone, the contrasts are fascinating. Here there are a potpourri of different designs, representing a host of styles, periods, and architectural preferences. The Union Station at Canaan (see pages 36–39)—largely destroyed by fire in October 2001—was a fine example of the Gothic Revival style. This three-story station, built in 1872, featured a tall tower, narrow arched windows, and board and batten siding; all strong vertical elements for which the Gothic Revival style is known. Not far away, in Waterbury, is a large brick station representative of the Renaissance Revival style. The state capitol at Hartford boasts a rugged looking brown stone Richardson Romanesque station designed by Shepley, Rutan and Coolidge (see pages 40–41). One of Richardson's own stations, in fact the last he designed, can be found at New London, Connecticut. This station is different from most of his other railroad stations because it is built of red brick, rather than the unfinished stone that was a Richardsonian trademark.

Dining at the Station

During the first few decades of railway travel, most passenger trains traveled relatively slowly and had few luxuries. The dining car wasn't developed for quite a few years. In the early days eating on the train usually meant a packed lunch. On many lines, long-distance trains would pause at strategic places where passengers could disembark for a half an hour or so and eat at a trackside restaurant that was often located in a railway station. These trackside oases needed to be a bit bigger than ordinary village stations, and tended to be located in places where the railroad needed to stop anyway, usually at division points, or places where locomotives were serviced. Unfortunately for the railroads, these trackside eateries gained a poor reputation and were widely criticized.

A British-born entrepeneur named Fred Harvey decided to provide high-quality trackside restaurants at an affordable price. He worked with the Santa Fe, a budding transcontinental railroad that connected Chicago and Kansas City with cities in Colorado and the Southwest. Eventually, Harvey operated a chain of restaurants along Santa Fe's lines that were known as Harvey Houses. He gradually expanded his business to include hotels as well. His establishments were famous not just for good service and fine food, but for his carefully selected employees: young, attractive, unmarried (a requirement for the job) women, known popularly as "Harvey Girls." While the Harvey restaurants and hotels have long since closed, several relatively large stations along the Santa Fe, such as those at Barstow, California,

(see pages 76–77) and Las Vegas, New Mexico (see pages 70–71), offer evidence of Harvey's business.

The development of the railroad dining car spelled the end for most railroad restaurants. Yet some survived at big stations where passengers made their connections and had time for a meal while waiting, and at railroad division points, where train crews could get a meal before heading out on a run or after finishing one.

Union Stations

In the early days, most American railroads were conceived as short lines that would simply connect the places in their names. For example, the Mohawk & Hudson did little more than form a bridge between its namesake rivers. Even railroads with grander names, such as the Baltimore & Ohio, took decades to connect the places they were named for, and in the case of the B&O, the railroad was originally only looking as far west as the Ohio River. Gradually lines were joined together and large railway systems began to emerge. By the 1870s, several large railways in the East had formed trunk lines that were directing the bulk of intercity traffic. As the railways grew, their services improved, and an ever-greater number of people traveled by train. At the same time America was also growing in size and population. Before the railroad boom in the 1830s, Chicago, a city often described as the "Railroad Capital" because of the large number of lines that met there, was an insignificant outpost with only a few dozen people living in it. By the turn of the last century Chicago's population had swelled to become one of America's largest cities in part due to its role as a transportation hub.

Railway competition was fierce, and during the height of the railroad building boom in the post-Civil War period, a town might suddenly find it was blessed with two or more railroads. However, often each company decided to build its own station. In many cases this led to great inconvenience to travelers, especially if the different railway stations were located on opposite sides of town.

The logical solution for railroads serving a common area was to build jointly operated stations at junctions and terminals that could serve two or more companies.

Above: Los Angeles Union Passenger Terminal was the last large railway terminal built in the United States. It was completed in 1939 and originally served the Santa Fe, Union Pacific, and Southern Pacific railroads. Today this handsome Art Deco structure is the terminal for Amtrak and Los Angeles Metro Link trains.

This had benefits for passengers and the railroads. Passengers got the convenience of easier connections and a choice of services, while the railroads could reduce their individual costs of maintaining a station. These jointly run stations are known in North America as union stations. In some cases a union station might be little more than a depot at a junction in the woods, while in others it might be the largest of big city terminals, served by more than a dozen different railroads.

Despite the advantages of building a union station, the railroads were often reluctant to make the investment, and it was typically the communities that forced the railroads to consolidate their facilities. The congestion caused by a multitude of railroads crossing each other and city streets a grade was a concern for cities, and many later union stations were designed as part of grade separation schemes aimed at getting the tracks off street level. In some cases, such as in Baltimore, the tracks were placed in cuts and in tunnels, but more often they were elevated on viaducts. The Worcester, Massachusetts, station had such tracks. When Worcester's beautiful new Union Station opened in 1911, all three of the city's railroads—the Boston & Albany, Boston & Maine, and New Haven—reached the station on grade-separated rights-of-way, an improvement that has benefited Worcester to this day.

The name Union Station can sometimes be deceiving. Some union stations were not as effective as they could have been. Chicago Union Station (pages 48–49) served just four of the many railroads that reached that city. In its heyday Chicago had a half a dozen major passenger terminals, and even today it has four major stations.

The Great Terminals

America's largest and most prosperous cities developed comprehensive railroad networks which required large terminals that could accommodate huge numbers of passengers. The railroads viewed these terminals as the companies' crown jewels, as showpieces of wealth, and as grand gates to the cities they served. The best architects in the country competed fiercely for big-city terminal commissions, and today the most renowned architects of the period are known for their terminals.

Above: The front portion of Boston's South Station escaped destruction in the mid-1970s when much of the station was demolished. The station has since been renovated and remodeled. Today it serves trains operated by Amtrak and the Massachusetts Bay Transportation Authority.

A passenger arriving at a large terminal during the railroads' heyday was besieged by a cacophony of sound and visual turmoil. Voices announced the departure of trains. Steam and smoke escaped from the locomotives as trains rolled in and out. Small trains of baggage carts pushed through waiting rooms and concourses, past the hordes of travelers making their way to trains.

A large terminal employed hundreds, sometimes thousands, of people: the Station Master who oversaw the operation; Red Caps who assisted travelers with their luggage; and ticket clerks who issued passage on the railway, to mention just a few. As trains left the terminal, they emerged from a great shed that shielded passengers from the elements and negotiated complex track arrangements of switches that sent them to their respective destinations. These switches were controlled by skilled signalmen in switching towers along the lines.

Boston was the first large city to have embraced a large suburban railway network allowing people to commute to work from outlying towns. Boston's South Station (see this page and pages 2 and 33), completed in 1898, was for many years the busiest station in America. It served the trains of three divisions of the New Haven Railroad and those of the Boston & Albany.

Eventually the new Grand Central Terminal (see pages vi, 10–11) in New York, completed in 1913 to replace the older Grand Central Station, overtook South Station as the busiest railway terminal in America. This magnificent building was the work of architects Reed & Stem and Warren & Watmore. The new Grand Central featured platforms on two levels that accessed 67 tracks, more than any other station in the world. Grand Central, like the new Pennsylvania Station a few blocks away, benefited from railroad electrification, which had been designed to eliminate the need for steam locomotives by using electricity to power the trains. At the time of the construction of these two great New York City terminals, their respective railroads—the New York Central and the Pennsylvania—were the two largest in the United States, and among the most richest and influential companies of their time. Each company wanted to outdo the other in the construction of a great New York terminal. Today we can look at Grand Central and admire its immense concourse, trace the patterns of the heavens on its vast arched ceiling, and feel inspired by the wonderful Beaux Arts architecture that has made it one of the best-known stations in the world. In its day, Pennsylvania Station, designed by McKim, Mead, and White, opened in 1910 and demolished in 1963, was an equally great architectural achievement.

Decline, Demolition, and Rebirth

The completion of the New York terminals was the zenith of American railway station architecture. Following World War I, American railroads began to face serious competition from other modes of transportation, and by the late 1920s, they had entered a long period of gradual decline as their business eroded. Despite this, some lines remained hopeful about the future of the passenger train, and several important terminals were constructed in the 1920s and 1930s, including a new Buffalo terminal and Cincinnati Union Station, both designed by Fellheimer and Wagner, and the Los Angeles Union Passenger Terminal, completed in 1939. The Pennsylvania Railroad's 30th Street Station in Philadelphia (see pages 14–15), completed in 1933, allowed the railroad to provide that city with a through terminal which greatly improved railroad service. Now 30th Street Station is among the busiest in the United States.

During the 1930s, American railroads curtailed many lightly patronized and unprofitable services, particularly secondary trains and those that served country branch lines. As result many small stations were closed to passengers, although some remained open as freight agencies and railroad operations centers. World War II saw a resurgence in rail travel, as America's war mobilization created a great need to get from place to place while severe restrictions on petroleum and rubber precluded most Americans from using automobiles for transport. During the war, many railroads carried more passengers than they had ever moved before. After the war, however, passenger counts and revenues plummeted. Many lines scrambled to attract riders by introducing fancy new trains and improved services. This had a modest effect during the 1950s, but the development of the interstate highway system and introduction of jet planes on passenger routes dealt a devastating blow to the railroads.

During the 1950s and 1960s many routes lost their passenger trains and hundreds of stations saw their last passengers depart. While smaller stations were often the first to go, many larger stations were destroyed as well. As part of this architectural slaughter, America lost one of its finest buildings. In 1963, the Pennsylvania Railroad demolished its highly acclaimed New York terminal, replacing the classic structure with a modern railroad terminal combined with the new Madison Square Garden. While the new building retained its function as a station, the grandeur was lost. The only good that came of this destruction was that the public outcry over the loss of Penn Station resulted in new laws that protect historic buildings.

By the early 1970s, America's largest rail-passenger carriers were looking to get out of the passenger business altogether and focus their efforts on freight services, the portion of railroading that generated most of their profits. In 1971, the federal government created Amtrak, a nationally-owned corporation which assumed operation of most remaining long distance passenger routes. With the changeover from private operations to Amtrak, roughly 50 percent of the passenger routes in America were discontinued, and numerous stations were closed. In a similar move, in the 1970s and 1980s, the operation of suburban passenger services was taken over from the private railroads by local public transportation authorities.

Although a great many railway stations were closed and abandoned and demolished following the loss of regular passenger train service, not all were destroyed. Some have survived as stations for Amtrak and commuter rail agencies, and others that had lain dormant for years have been restored to service. In the last few decades, many large cities, such as Boston, New York, Chicago and Los Angeles, have developed thriving suburban commuter rail networks. As a result some traditional stations have regained daily passenger services, although it's more common for new commuter lines to serve newly-built, modern facilities. Other stations have been renovated and used for a great variety of purposes and today, hundreds of beautifully restored railroad stations can be found all across America. So while the station may not be the vital community center it was in the past, the railway station lives on, and its history is part of us.

Opposite: Grand Central's famous 42nd Street façade was designed by Reed & Stem, Minnesota-based architects who had worked on many lesser-known stations. Grand Central was the New York Central line's gift to the city, and it is certainly one of the finest stations ever built.

❖

Above: Artwork on the ceiling of Grand Central's lower level embraces a railroad theme.

❖

Left: The bronze chandeliers in Grand Central's waiting room are just one of the fine touches that give the station its legendary magnificence.

Lackawanna's Hoboken Terminal, opened in 1907, was designed by Kenneth W. Murchison to replace an early terminal destroyed by fire. This elaborate station complex was one of several large railway stations on the west shore of the Hudson River across from New York City. Like the other waterfront railway terminals, it included ferry facilities to allow passengers to walk directly from trains to boats that would bring them across the river to Manhattan. Today the terminal is operated by New Jersey Transit.

Above and opposite, bottom: The Pennsylvania Railroad's 30th Street Station was one of the last great terminals built in the United States. Opened on March 12, 1933, it uses a through track arrangement designed to improve long distance passenger service through Philadelphia. The station's impressive Neoclassic design draws heavily on Greek influences, as evidence by its massive Corinthian colonnade. In the late 1980s Amtrak renovated the station, restoring its former glory and making it again one of the showpieces of American railroad architecture. It is one of the busiest terminals on Amtrak's Northeast Corridor.

Opposite, top: In the nineteenth century most large railway stations featured trainsheds to keep the wind and the rain from bothering passengers as they boarded trains. One of the more common types of shed used a truss frame, such as this one in Harrisburg, Pennsylvania. This shed is now one of the last in regular use in the United States.

Pages 16-17: The Western Maryland railroad had both offices and a moderately sized depot at its Union Bridge, Maryland, station. Today this building serves as the office for the Western Maryland Historical Society and the headquarters for the Maryland Midland, a shortline railroad operating on a section of the old Western Maryland mainline.

Above and left: Baltimore's Mt. Royal Station was designed by E. Francis Baldwin and Josias Pennington. Baldwin was responsible for many railway buildings on the Baltimore & Ohio. This Romanesque station was built in conjunction with a tunnel through downtown that was designed to ease railway traffic flow on the Baltimore & Ohio Railroad. Mt. Royal Station, along with the Harrisburg station (see page 15) is one of the few remaining American railway stations that retains its traditional shed.

Opposite: The brick station at Perryville, Maryland, was built in 1905 in a Colonial Revival style. Today it is a suburban passenger stop between Baltimore and Philadelphia along the busy Northeast Corridor.

Right: Baltimore & Ohio's station at Brunswick, Maryland, glows in the last light of an October evening. This station was built in 1891 and like many others on the B&O, was the work of E. Francis Baldwin and Josias Pennington. It still serves as a railway station for MARC commuter trains.

Pages 22-23: Washington Union Station was designed to consolidate railroad facilities and help improve the appearance of America's capitol city. The building was the work of Daniel H. Burnham, who designed other acclaimed stations, including the Pennsylvania Railroad's Pittsburgh station. He was also responsible for designing the 1893 Columbian Exposition in Chicago; Union Station incorporates some architectural elements from that project. In the 1970s this majestic station was allowed to deteriorate and was closed to the public in 1981. Seven years later it reopened following a multi-million dollar restoration.

Above: Washington Union Station features an impressive 96-foot-tall barrel vault roof.

Opposite: Among the station's Classical features are the 36 statues of Roman Legionnaires.

Right: Completed in 1911, the Worcester (Massachusetts) Union Station was built to serve the Boston & Albany, Boston & Maine, and New Haven Railroads. It was designed by Samuel Huckel, Jr., and built in conjunction with a grade separation program to put the busy railway lines above street level. The station was closed in 1972 and lay derelict for more than two decades, but in the late 1990s it underwent a multi-million dollar restoration.

❖

Below: Prior to its restoration, the once grand station was a sad commentary on the decline of the American railway network and urban decay that blighted so many Northeastern cities.

Left and above: The restoration of Worcester Union Station included the reconstruction of its two large towers, which had been demolished decades earlier for structural reasons, and the refurbishing of its ceiling, complete with cleaned and repaired skylights.

Warren, Massachusetts, is one of several villages located along the Boston & Albany in the Quaboag River Valley. Warren's handsome brownstone station—one of several along the line designed by Shepley, Rutan and Coolidge—is neatly located in a small park at the center of town. Today the station serves as office for a private business, and the trains roll by without stopping.

Above: Palmer, Massachusetts, is a small town on the old Boston & Albany that was blessed with a handsome station designed by Henry Hobson Richardson, and completed in 1884. At the time, Richardson was one of America's foremost architects. He was also one of the first Americans to attend the École des Beaux-Arts in France. While the station still stands, passenger trains haven't picked up riders here regularly since the 1960s.

❖

Opposite: Boston's South Station is still a busy rail hub, yet little of the original 1898 Shepley, Rutan and Coolidge station remains beyond the Atlantic Avenue and Summer Street façade. The station's Romanesque design contrasts with the modern skyscrapers that surround it. Like so many big city terminals, South Station was designed to awe the traveler, but today it is lost in a sea of architectural discordance.

Opposite: One of the most distinctive railway stations in New England is the old Boston & Maine station at North Conway, New Hampshire. It was built in 1874 in a Russian style that seems incongruous considering its bucolic White Mountains setting. However, North Conway has been a popular resort for more than a century, and this oddly eclectic depot was designed for the holiday traveler. Today it serves the Conway Scenic Railway.

Above: In the shadow of the White Mountains, the classic brick depot at Groveton, New Hampshire, sits at the junction of the old Grand Trunk and Boston & Maine lines, neither of which has seen a scheduled passenger train in decades. Both are now operated by new shortline freight lines. The station is fond reminder of the glory days of railway travel.

Pages 36-37: The Union Station at Canaan, Connecticut, was a classic example of Victorian Gothic Revival architecture that was popular in the New England region in the mid-nineteenth century. The station, which was located in the far northwest corner of the state, was built in 1872 to serve the north-south Housatonic Railroad and the east-west Connecticut Western. Both of these lines ultimately became part of the New Haven Railroad. Although it was no longer a regular passenger station, the building housed railroad offices and other businesses until it was destroyed by a fire in October, 2001.

The Canaan Union Station featured a three-story tower topped by a weather vane in the shape of a steam locomotive.

Above and right: Hartford Union Station sits just a few blocks from the Connecticut State Capitol. This magnificent Romanesque building was designed by George Keller and Shepley, Rutan and Coolidge. Completed in 1889, it suffered from neglect in the 1960s and 1970s but was restored in 1987.

Above and opposite: This modern station at Providence, Rhode Island, incorporates several of the traditional features found in classic railroad station design, including the prominent clock tower and eave-supporting colonnades. Sitting in the shadow of the state capitol, the station was built in 1986 in conjunction with a line relocation through the center of the city. Today it is an important stop for Amtrak's *Acela Express* and also hosts Boston area commuter trains.

❧

Pages 44-45: Bellows Falls, Vermont, was an historic railroad junction where the Rutland Railroad met the Boston & Maine and Central Vermont. Today the station is still served by passenger trains of both Amtrak and the privately run Green Mountain Railroad. In this misty morning view, the passenger station is seen on the right, the Green Mountain's dispatchers office is in the center, and the freight station (since destroyed) is on the left.

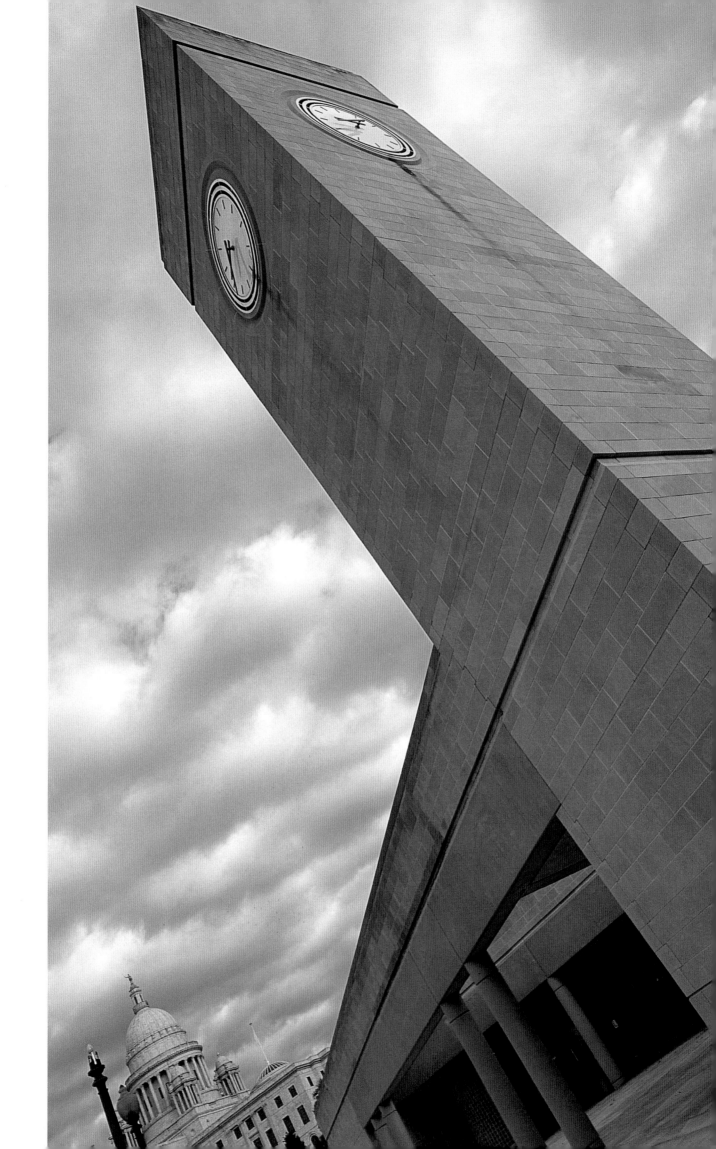

HIGHL

Opposite: In the fall of 1964, a Boston & Maine conductor waits to greet passengers on the platform of the Bellows Falls station.

Above: Highlands Station at Hinsdale, Illinois, was built as a 'flag' stop, a place where trains would only stop on request. While most flag stops only used simple shelters, Highlands received a handsome stone station building. Today this little station is still served by Chicago's Metra suburban passenger carrier.

Above and opposite: Chicago Union Station was built in 1925 to serve the Pennsylvania Railroad; the Burlington, Milwaukee Road; and the Alton. The station was designed by Graham, Anderson, Probst and White, and is noted for its spacious waiting room with immense skylights. Unfortunately, the station's acclaimed concourse was destroyed in 1969.

Left and below: Joliet Union Station was built in 1911 to consolidate four separate railway stations and elevate the tracks through this busy Chicago satellite. The unusually shaped station was designed by Jarvis Hunt, and it shares architectural elements with the 16th Street Station in Oakland, California, another Hunt design (see pages 80-81). Joliet Union Station was restored in 1991 following decades of neglect.

Pages 52-53: Indianapolis Union Station is a fine example of late nineteenth-century Romanesque architecture. When it was completed in 1888 it was a Midwestern passenger hub. Indianapolis is now served by only one passenger train daily, so in 1986 this grand old station was converted into a railway theme hotel and office complex.

JOLIET

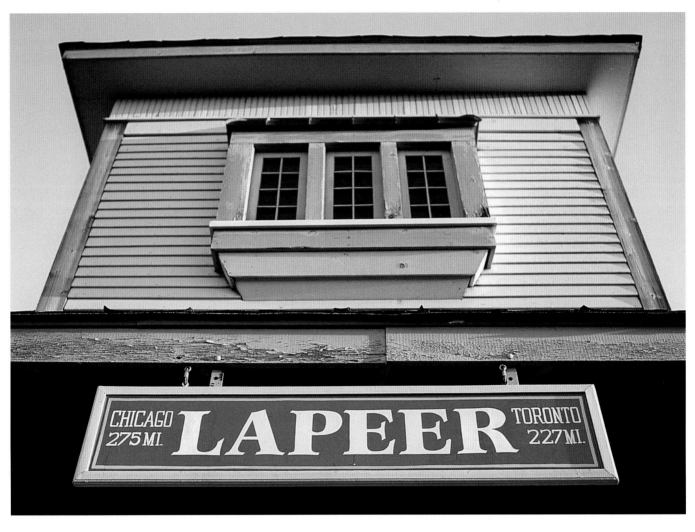

Left: The clock tower is an important element of many railroad stations. This was especially true in the days when railroad standard time was different from the local "sun time" used by most communities. This Romanesque tower is part of Indianapolis Union Station.

❖

Above: Lapeer, Michigan, lies roughly midway between Chicago and Toronto on the Grand Trunk Western. This small town station is a stop for Amtrak's *International*, which runs daily between the two main terminals on the line.

❖

Pages 56-57: The sun rises over the Grand Trunk Western tracks at Lapeer, Michigan. The classic wood frame depot on the left and grain elevators on the right are typical of hundreds of small agricultural towns throughout the midwestern United States.

A thick spring fog shrouds the depot at Brookfield, Wisconsin, along the old Milwaukee Road main line to the Twin Cities, Minneapolis and St. Paul, both in Minnesota. Depots such as this one were often basic utilitarian structures built to standard plans. The size of the station depended on how much business the railroad felt a town along the line would generate.

Above: The steam-powered passenger train passing a country station was once a common scene that occurred tens of thousands of times daily all across America. The railway station at North Freedom, Wisconsin, is a re-creation of a typical Midwestern country depot. The station itself formerly resided along the Chicago & North Western a few miles away at Rock Springs.

❧

Pages 60-61: The stone and brick depot at Whitewater, Wisconsin, was built from a standard plan by architect John T.W. Jennings in 1890 to replace an earlier station. Whitewater is a college town along an old Milwaukee Road line that is now operated by the Wisconsin Southern.

Below: Omaha, Nebraska's Union Station was the work of Gilbert S. Underword. Completed in 1931, it remains an excellent display of Art Deco style. Today the station is owned by the city and home to the Durham Western Heritage Museum.

❧

Right: Only a block away from Omaha Union Station was the Burlington's station, a much older facility that dated to 1889. Like Union Station, the depot building is at street level, while the tracks are on a lower level. This Greek Revival building was heavily modified in the early 1930s.

❧

Pages 64-65: Great Northern's large depot and divisional office building at Whitefish, Montana, is situated at the western base of Marias Pass. Its design emulates that of a Swiss chalet, which seems appropriate for a depot located in the Rocky Mountains. The building was built in 1927 to replace an earlier depot on the site.

MUSEUM PARKING 7'-6" CLEAR

OMAHA UNION STATION

DURHAM WESTERN HERITAGE MUSEUM

— DURHAM —
Western Heritage
Museum

Opposite: The old Great Northern Station at Whitefish, Montana, is a classic example of a station at a remote division point where a larger facility was required to house and feed crews and serve as office space.

❖

Above: Railroads would often place stations at strategic points for operational reasons, even if the local population was too small to warrant a passenger stop. This small station is along the old Rio Grande narrow gauge at the top of Cumbres Pass, more than 10,000 feet above sea level, in the Colorado Rockies.

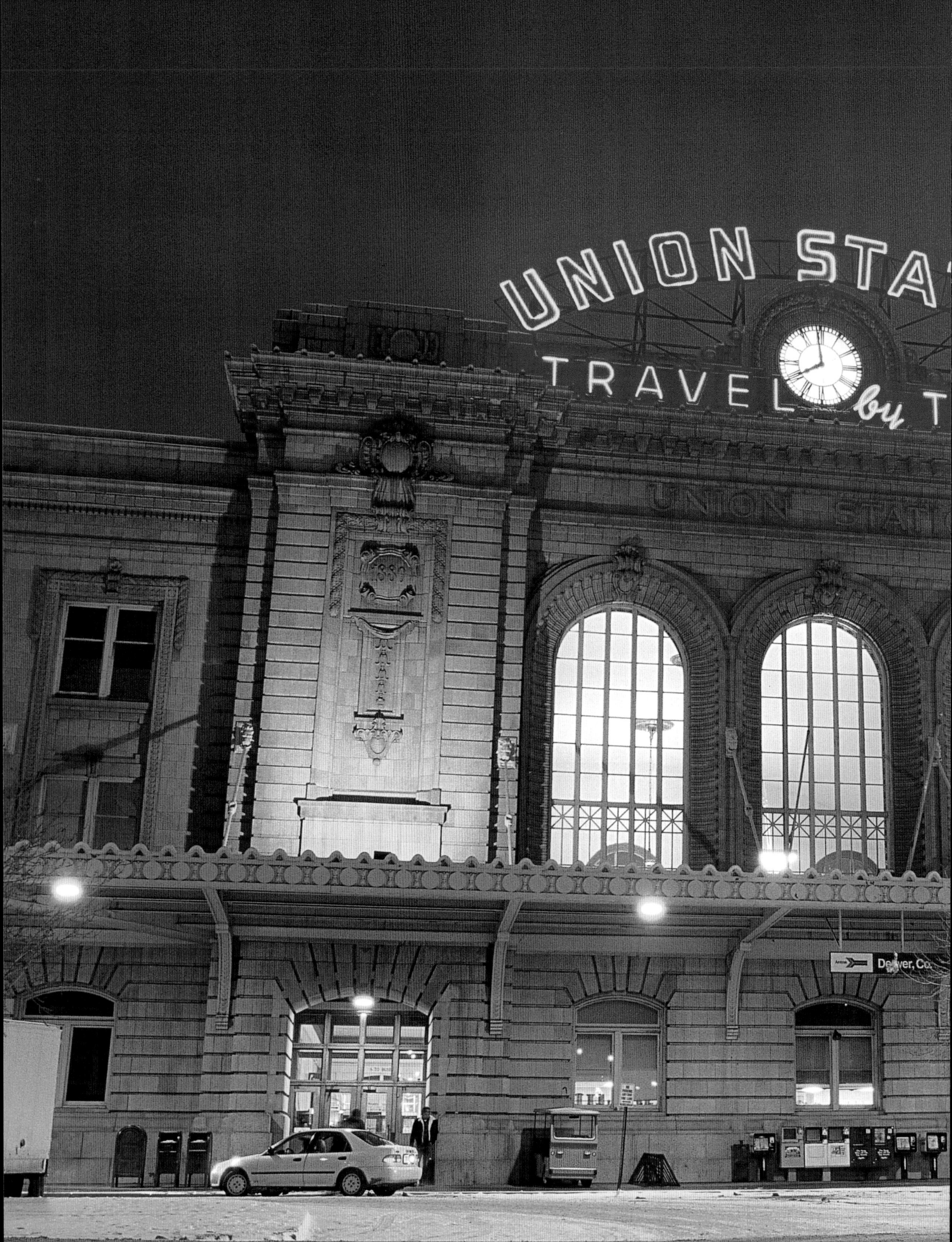
UNION STA
TRAVEL by T
Denver, Co.

Denver Union Station was once served by a half dozen different railroads. As late as the 1960s, Denver Union was a major passenger hub. Today only Amtrak's *California Zephyr* uses the station on a daily basis. The station was originally built in 1881, but it has been significantly rebuilt and modified since that time.

Opposite, left, and below: Strategically situated at the base of Glorieta Pass, Las Vegas, New Mexico, was an important railroad center on the Santa Fe. In addition to having a handsome depot, Las Vegas is the location of the old Casteñeda Hotel, one of several hotels originally run by Fred Harvey, British-born restaurant and hotel magnate who provided eateries and accommodations along the Santa Fe. It was designed by Frederic L. Roehrig in the Spanish Mission style. Although closed in the 1940s, the building is a handsome reminder of the Santa Fe's glory days.

Pages 72-73: Santa Fe's Raton, New Mexico, station dates from 1904. This Spanish Mission-style building once contained a Harvey House restaurant and an elaborate spire once adorned the top of the tower. Harvey House restaurants took pride in their high-quality, consistent pricing and attractive friendly waitresses. Harvey restaurants and hotels often served railroad train crews in addition to passengers, especially at remote locations such as Raton, where the station is at the base of Santa Fe's Raton Pass crossing. Amtrak still serves Raton with its daily *Southwest Chief*.

Above: Traditionally railroads encouraged the planting of gardens and flower beds around stations to improve their appearance. This custom has been maintained at the former Northwestern Pacific depot in Petaluma, California.

Opposite: Many Western railways were directly responsible for the creation of towns along their lines, and the railways often named new towns after their officials. Perris, California, was named for Santa Fe's chief civil engineer, Frederick Perris. The station, built in 1892, was the work of Perris' son-in-law, Benjamin F. Levet.

Left: Santa Fe's 1911-built Barstow, California, station included a Fred Harvey hotel and restaurant. This station was designed by California architect Francis W. Wilson. Barstow is situated northeast of Los Angeles and has long been an important junction on the Santa Fe and the location of a large yard.

Pages 78-79: This handsome Spanish Colonial style building at Alturas, California, was the station and offices for the Nevada-California-Oregon, a narrow gauge railway that traversed the sparsely populated Modoc region of northern California, connecting Reno, Nevada, with Lakeview, Oregon.

Opposite, left, and below: Southern Pacific's gray granite depot at 16th Street in Oakland, California, may seem something of an architectural anomaly for a west coast terminal, but it is appropriate for a city that as a major industrial base and international shipping center has more in common with the big east coast ports than most cities in California. It was designed by Jarvis Hunt, who was also responsible for a similar railroad station in Joliet, Illinois (see pages 50-51).

The former Southern Pacific station at Davis, California, is located at the junction of the transcontinental line to the Bay Area and the lightly used West Valley line that heads towards Oregon. Today this classic Spanish style depot is served by more than a dozen Amtrak trains daily.

Above, opposite, and pages 86-87: Sacramento, California, was the original western terminus of the first transcontinental railroad. The former Southern Pacific station in Sacramento is a handsome, conservatively-designed building completed in 1926 and located a few blocks west of downtown. The Southern Pacific Line was a myriad of companies that connected many points in California and throughout the West. The station is now served by more than a dozen daily Amtrak trains. A large mural in the station depicts the famous ground-breaking ceremony held in 1863 for this strategic railroad route.

Index